C. J. STROUD

FOOTBALL SUPERSTAR

BY ANTHONY K. HEWSON

Copyright © 2025 by Press Room Editions. All rights reserved. No part of this book may be used or reproduced in any manner whatsoever, including internet usage, without written permission from the copyright owner, except in the case of brief quotations embodied in critical articles and reviews.

Book design by Jake Nordby
Cover design by Jake Nordby

Photographs ©: Paul Jasienski/AP Images, cover, 1; Bob Levey/Getty Images Sport/Getty Images, 4–5; Cooper Neill/AP Images, 6; Louis Lopez/Cal Sport Media/Newscom, 8; Louis Lopez/Cal Sport Media/AP Images, 11; David Chisholm/Image of Sport/AP Images, 13; Mike Stobe/Getty Images Sport/Getty Images, 14; Ben Jackson/Getty Images Sport/Getty Images, 16; Carmen Mandato/Getty Images Sport/Getty Images, 19; Logan Bowles/AP Images, 20, 30; Dylan Buell/Getty Images Sport/Getty Images, 23; Michael Owens/Getty Images Sport/Getty Images, 24; Michael Owens/AP Images, 26–27; Red Line Editorial, 29

Press Box Books, an imprint of Press Room Editions, Inc.

ISBN
978-1-63494-933-0 (library bound)
978-1-63494-938-5 (paperback)
978-1-63494-947-7 (epub)
978-1-63494-943-9 (hosted ebook)

Library of Congress Control Number: 2024939614

Distributed by North Star Editions, Inc.
2297 Waters Drive
Mendota Heights, MN 55120
www.northstareditions.com

Printed in the United States of America
082024

About the Author
Anthony K. Hewson is a freelance writer originally from San Diego. He and his wife now live in San Francisco with their two dogs.

TABLE OF CONTENTS

CHAPTER 1
Comeback Kid 5

CHAPTER 2
Through Hard Times 9

CHAPTER 3
Becoming a Buckeye 15

CHAPTER 4
Instant Success 21

SPECIAL FEATURE
All Day to Throw 26

Timeline • 28
At a Glance • 30
Glossary • 31
To Learn More • 32
Index • 32

1 COMEBACK KID

Houston Texans fans were stunned. The Tampa Bay Buccaneers had just taken a 37-33 lead with 46 seconds left. To win the game, the Texans would have to drive 75 yards and score a touchdown.

C. J. Stroud calmly took the field. The Texans quarterback was in the middle of a great rookie season. Stroud was known for keeping his cool under pressure. And he threw extremely accurate passes. He would have to do both to lead the Texans to a comeback win.

C. J. Stroud had thrown nine touchdown passes and one interception in his first seven NFL games.

Stroud (7) celebrates with a teammate after tossing a touchdown pass against Tampa Bay.

Stroud completed his first three passes of the drive. Houston was now on Tampa Bay's side of the field. But the Texans were out of timeouts with only 16 seconds left. Stroud then delivered a 26-yard pass to Tank Dell between two defenders.

Just 10 seconds remained. From the 15-yard line, Stroud dropped back to pass. He calmly scanned the field. Then he fired a rocket of a pass to Dell. The rookie wide receiver caught it for a touchdown. The crowd erupted in celebration.

The win improved Houston's record to 4–4. The Texans hadn't won more than four games in the previous three seasons. But that was before the team drafted Stroud. With the calm quarterback leading the team, winning always seemed possible.

MAKING HISTORY

In the win against the Buccaneers, Stroud passed for 470 yards. No rookie had ever thrown for that many yards in a game before. Stroud also became the third quarterback in National Football League (NFL) history to throw five touchdown passes with no interceptions in a game.

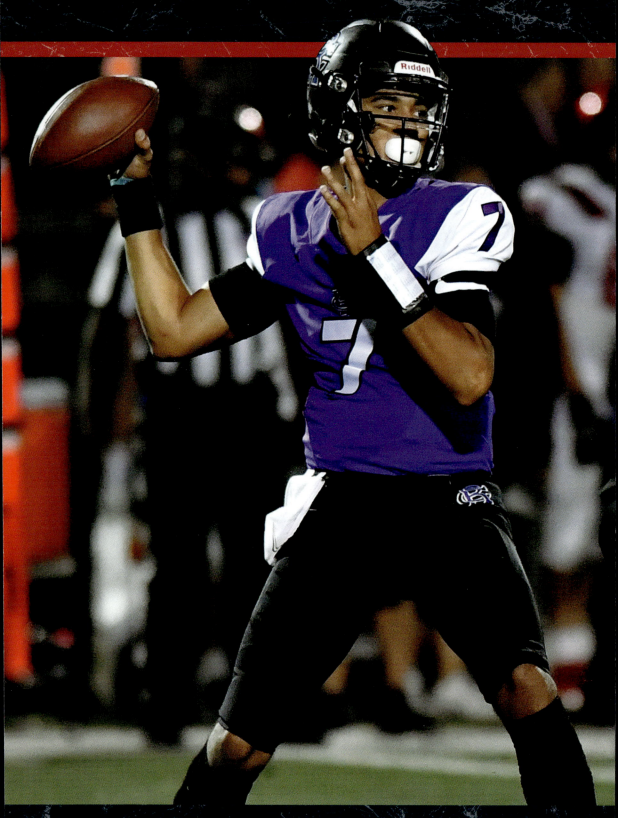

2 THROUGH HARD TIMES

C. J. Stroud was born on October 3, 2001. He grew up in Rancho Cucamonga, California. His family raised him to be competitive. There was a basketball hoop in the backyard of his house. C. J. and his three siblings played against one another all the time. C. J. was the youngest by seven years. And his siblings didn't go easy on him. Even so, C. J. always wanted to compete.

C. J. played baseball, basketball, and soccer, too. But his first love was

On top of football, C. J. Stroud played on his high school varsity basketball team for two years.

WHY C. J.?

C. J. was named after his father. His full name is Coleridge Bernard Stroud IV. But he goes by "C. J." The *C* stands for his first name. He has never said where the *J* comes from. C. J.'s family sometimes calls him by his nickname, "Cool Breeze." C. J. got that name for always being calm and cool.

football. His dad, Coleridge, introduced him to football when he was five. Coleridge also taught his son almost everything he knew about playing quarterback.

Football ended up being C. J.'s best sport. But Coleridge wasn't able to see his son become a star. When C. J. was 13, his father went to prison. C. J.'s mother, Kimberly, had to raise four kids by herself. She could not afford to stay in their home. Instead, the family moved multiple times before ending up in a two-bedroom apartment.

C. J. Stroud ran for 328 yards and six touchdowns during his high school career.

Without his dad to teach him, C. J. found other ways to learn about playing quarterback. He studied videos of quarterbacks he admired. C. J. especially loved watching highlights of New Orleans Saints legend Drew Brees. He also had great coaches. As a freshman in high school, C. J. made the varsity team. But he didn't start a game until his junior year. When C. J. won the starting job, he battled through injuries. Few colleges were interested in him after his junior year.

C. J. worked hard to improve before his senior year. He attended off-season camps. He competed with some of the top quarterback recruits in the country. Scouts at the camps thought C. J. looked better than his peers.

The hard work paid off. C. J. passed for 3,878 yards and 47 touchdowns in his senior

C. J. Stroud (center) puts on an Ohio State hat to announce his plan to play football for the Buckeyes.

season. Those stats caught the attention of major college football programs. Almost every school wanted C. J. He had offers from top programs like Georgia, Michigan, and Oregon. He chose to attend Ohio State University.

3 BECOMING A BUCKEYE

There were many quarterbacks C. J. Stroud looked up to. One was Justin Fields. In October 2019, Stroud got to meet Fields on a visit to Ohio State. Fields was Ohio State's starting quarterback at the time. He helped convince Stroud to play for the Buckeyes. Fields hoped Stroud would continue Ohio State's long history of success.

By January 2020, Stroud had finished high school early. So, he moved to the Ohio State campus. That fall, Stroud got

Stroud threw for 4,435 yards in his first year as a starter for Ohio State.

Stroud threw 85 touchdowns and 12 interceptions with the Buckeyes.

to learn from Fields as his backup. Fields left for the NFL before the 2021 season. That gave Stroud a chance to play. He won the starting job by being accurate and making good decisions. Ohio State head coach, Ryan Day, also thought Stroud showed great leadership.

Day ended up being right. In 2021, Stroud completed more than 70 percent of his throws. He tossed 44 touchdown passes and only six interceptions. Stroud led the Buckeyes to a 10-2 record. The team also earned a trip to the Rose Bowl.

The Buckeyes struggled early in the Rose Bowl. After the first quarter, they trailed Utah 14-0. Stroud rallied with three long touchdown passes in the second quarter. But the Buckeyes still trailed by 14 at halftime.

Early in the second half, Stroud threw an interception. However, he kept his team in the game. He tossed three more touchdowns in the second half. The game was tied with less than two minutes left. Stroud then marched the Buckeyes down the field. They kicked a late field goal to win the game.

GIVING BACK

C. J. Stroud earned a lot of money in college by promoting products for companies. In fact, he was one of the highest-paid college athletes in the country. Stroud spent some of the money on a new car. He gave some money to teammates, too. His biggest expense was for his family, though. Stroud bought a new house for his mom and sister.

Fans expected Stroud to be even better the next year. Once again, he delivered. Stroud posted great numbers. He led Ohio State to the College Football Playoff. That gave the Buckeyes a chance to play for a national championship.

Ohio State faced Georgia in the semifinals. The Bulldogs were the defending national champions. Also, the game took place in Atlanta, Georgia. The tough Georgia defense would be Stroud's biggest test yet. But Stroud had little trouble against the Bulldogs. He passed for 348 yards and four touchdowns.

Ohio State's 41 points were 11 more than any other team scored on Georgia in 2022.

However, the Buckeyes defense allowed a late touchdown. Ohio State lost a heartbreaker 42–41.

Stroud had a decision to make after the season. He could come back to school for another shot at a national title. Or he could head to the NFL. Stroud decided to go pro.

4 INSTANT SUCCESS

The Carolina Panthers had the top pick in the 2023 NFL Draft. They desperately needed a franchise quarterback. And they were in luck. Carolina had two talented quarterbacks to choose from. Alabama's Bryce Young was one. C. J. Stroud was the other.

The Panthers chose Young. With the second pick, the Houston Texans drafted Stroud. He set out to prove that the Panthers had made the wrong choice.

Stroud threw for 242 yards in his NFL debut.

Texans fans wanted to see Stroud play. But not all rookie quarterbacks are ready to start in the NFL right away. The team told Stroud he'd have to earn the starting job. He embraced that challenge. Stroud impressed the coaches in practice. Before the season began, the Texans named Stroud their starter.

Stroud struggled in his first two starts. He didn't throw a touchdown pass until Week 2. And the Texans lost his first two games. Even so, Stroud showed signs of maturity. He didn't throw an interception until Week 6. Stroud set an NFL record

FAMOUS FRIEND

There wasn't much of a rivalry between the top two picks of the 2023 NFL Draft. C. J. Stroud and Bryce Young both grew up in Southern California. They had competed against each other since middle school. Then they became friends after high school. The quarterbacks got to face off in the NFL during their rookie seasons. Young and the Panthers won 15–13.

Stroud ran for three touchdowns during his rookie year.

for pass attempts without an interception to begin a career. Rookie quarterbacks often make mistakes and bad decisions. But Stroud rarely did. He showed an elite ability to be consistent and accurate.

Stroud completed 16 of his 21 pass attempts in his playoff debut.

Stroud quickly turned the Texans into playoff contenders. Their fate came down to the last game of the regular season. The Texans traveled to Indianapolis to play the Colts. The winner would clinch a spot in the playoffs.

Stroud started the game with a bang. On his first throw, he unleashed a deep bomb to Nico Collins. The receiver caught it for a 75-yard touchdown. In the biggest game of the season, Stroud wasn't fazed at all. He threw only six incompletions and had no turnovers. Houston won 23–19. That earned the Texans a home playoff game in front of their thrilled fans.

In his playoff debut, Stroud impressed again. He threw for 274 yards and three touchdowns. The Texans crushed the Cleveland Browns 45–14. Stroud became the youngest quarterback ever to start and win a playoff game.

Houston's run ended in the next round. Texans fans were disappointed in the moment. But they knew they had a star quarterback to watch for years to come.

ALL DAY TO THROW

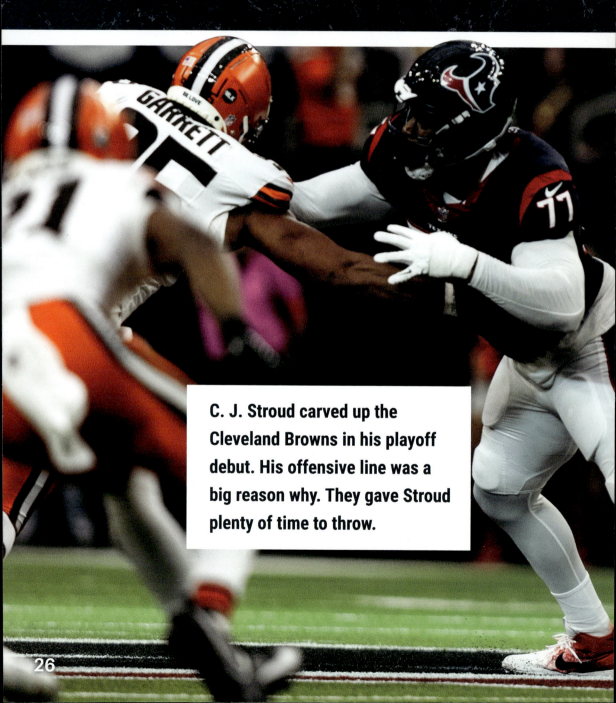

C. J. Stroud carved up the Cleveland Browns in his playoff debut. His offensive line was a big reason why. They gave Stroud plenty of time to throw.

TIMELINE

1. Rancho Cucamonga, California (October 3, 2001)
C. J. Stroud is born.

2. Minneapolis, Minnesota (September 2, 2021)
Stroud makes his first start for Ohio State.

3. Pasadena, California (January 1, 2022)
Stroud sets Rose Bowl records with 573 passing yards and six touchdown passes.

4. Atlanta, Georgia (December 31, 2022)
Stroud throws four touchdown passes against the defending national champion Georgia Bulldogs in the semifinals of the College Football Playoff. However, Ohio State loses 42-41.

5. Kansas City, Missouri (April 27, 2023)
The Houston Texans select Stroud with the second pick in the 2023 NFL Draft.

6. Baltimore, Maryland (September 10, 2023)
Stroud makes his NFL debut.

7. Indianapolis, Indiana (January 6, 2024)
Stroud leads the Texans to a win over the Indianapolis Colts and clinches a home playoff game.

8. Houston, Texas (January 13, 2024)
Stroud makes his playoff debut, leading the Texans to a win over the Cleveland Browns. He sets a record for most passing touchdowns by a rookie in a playoff game.

MAP

AT A GLANCE

Birth date: October 3, 2001

Birthplace: Rancho Cucamonga, California

Position: Quarterback

Throws: Right

Size: 6-foot-3 (191 cm), 218 pounds (99 kg)

NFL team: Houston Texans (2023–)

College team: Ohio State Buckeyes (2020–22)

Major awards: Big Ten Conference Offensive Player of the Year (2021–22), NFL Offensive Rookie of the Year (2023), Pro Bowl (2023)

Accurate through the 2023 season.

GLOSSARY

debut
First appearance.

drafted
Selected an athlete in an event that allows teams to choose new players coming into the league.

elite
The best of the best.

franchise quarterback
A quarterback capable of leading a team for many years.

freshman
A first-year student.

recruits
Athletes who college teams are interested in.

rookie
A first-year player.

scouts
People who look for talented young players.

turnovers
Plays where the offensive team loses the ball to the other team through an interception or fumble.

varsity
The top team in a sport at a high school.

TO LEARN MORE

Books

Lowe, Alexander. *G.O.A.T. Football Quarterbacks*. Minneapolis: Lerner Publications, 2023.

Mattern, Joanne. *Houston Texans*. Minneapolis: Bellwether Media, 2024.

Whiting, Jim. *The Story of the Houston Texans*. Mankato, MN: Creative Education, 2025.

More Information

To learn more about C. J. Stroud, go to **pressboxbooks.com/AllAccess**.

These links are routinely monitored and updated to provide the most current information available.

INDEX

Brees, Drew, 12

Carolina Panthers, 21–22
Cleveland Browns, 25–26
College Football Playoff, 18–19
Collins, Nico, 25

Day, Ryan, 16–17
Dell, Tank, 7

Fields, Justin, 15–16

Indianapolis Colts, 24

New Orleans Saints, 12
NFL Draft, 21–22

Rose Bowl, 17

Stroud, Coleridge, 10, 12

Stroud, Kimberly, 10, 18

Tampa Bay Buccaneers, 5–7

University of Alabama, 21
University of Georgia, 13, 18
University of Utah, 17

Young, Bryce, 21–22

32